AF260800

Sixtus Xystus VI

THE 666 ANTICHRIST SPIRIT REVEALED

JEFFREY CLEMENS

Copyright © 2026 Jeffrey Clemens.

All rights reserved. This book or any portion thereof may not be reproduced or used in any manner whatsoever without the express written permission of the publisher except for the use of brief quotation in a book review.

ISBN: 978-1-971940-41-0 (sc)
ISBN: 978-1-971940-42-7 (e)

Rev. date: 03/10/2026

CONTENTS

CONTEXT 1

AUTHOR'S NOTE TO THE THIRD EDITION 7

FOREWORD 11

INTRODUCTION 13

THE WAR FOR WORSHIP 15

MISSION 19

THE SIGN OF JONAH 21

THE GREATEST GENERATION 23

MY VISION 27

INTERPRETATION 31

SIXTUS XYSTUS VI THE 666 33

WARS AND RUMORS OF WARS 37

A NEW HOLY ROMAN EMPIRE 39

BY PEACE HE SHALL DESTROY 41

FALSE SIGNS AND WONDERS 43

THE TEMPLE 45

POSITIVE ID MICROCHIPS 47

TRIBULATION, RAPTURE, & THE SECOND COMING
OF JESUS CHRIST 51

JESUS IS OUR COMING OF TRUTH 56

CONTEXT

For our struggle is not against flesh and blood, but
against the rulers, against the powers, against the
world forces of this darkness, against the spiritual
forces of wickedness in the heavenly places.
Ephesians 6:12

MY FIRST BOOK "A COMING OF TRUTH" has been updated and retitled "Sixtus Xystus VI." This account is of the supernatural. It was generated by the Holy Spirit after the death of Pope John Paul II in 2005.

The vision came to me on the evening of 19 April 2005 after Pope Benedict XVI had announced himself. I was on leave at the time from the Defense Language Institute in California. I was visiting my friend Bill Overstreet of Roanoke, Virginia; a World War II fighter pilot. The impressions that came to me took place in Bill's brick Cape Cod home.

I reflected on what was granted to me for an entire year. In 2006 I committed it to writing while stationed at an austere post in South Korea. It was the most negative year of my adult life. During the construction of this account, I was under constant demonic attack. I had never experienced so much evil in all of my years in the ministry.

The city of Gwang-Ju was the site of a bloody massacre in 1980. We lived under severe restrictions with protestors constantly at our gate. I was literally driven to my knees for 11 months in prayer while stationed at our airfield. To survive this experience, I fervently prayed each morning and night at the base's Catholic Chapel for a solid hour.

The command environment that I was posted to was toxic. We had the highest suicide attempt rate on any base in theater. I once intercepted a shooter on his way to kill my crazed First Sergeant. My Soldiers were beaten down. One Soldier would be struck and killed by lightning. Things were so bad that 8th Army eventually had to move us to another site.

In The Revelation To John we are told that each Church has an angel posted over it. I did not have to be in Ephesus to be under the watch of the angelic host. My constant prayers for the well-being of my Soldiers under spiritual duress would be rewarded in a simple Army chapel by an angelic presence.

In late 2006 I would have an angel manifest itself to me after a heavy round of prayer at the Religious Retreat Center Chapel in Seoul. It was late at night. I had just stood to relieve my numbed knees. As I was turning to my left, I then became aware of a light at the front of the darkened chapel. I stole a glance. Before me at an elevated position stood the energy form of an angel.

It looked like it was composed of a cloud of bright white. Its face was a ball of light. I could perceive its wings held upright close to its torso. Its human-like form was covered in a full-length vestment.

The figure was approximately six feet tall. There were no feet under the hem of it's garment. I beheld its reassuring presence for a brief moment. Then it vanished before my eyes like a light bulb being suddenly switched off.

This divine contact was made in silence. No words were necessary. I had a mission to fulfill by recording the vision which God had granted me. This apparition confirmed it.

My first tour in South Korea would be a major testing ground. It was as close to an actual war that you could get without declaring one. My struggle was further amplified by even darker forces from the lower spiritual realm. It would take me two years to recover from this beating.

Upon my return home, I shared my manuscript with my very wise and close friend Bill Overstreet. I had announced a man as the Devil. I was then warned to wait a year until I published the manuscript. Bill knew that the Army would view me as a threat for releasing this material. Despite a very high record of service, this account would ultimately cost me my chaplaincy and almost my life.

In the ancient days men fought battles in chariots. Bill's generation was the first to fight in the stratosphere with combat aircraft. It was only fitting that part of my vision would include aircraft from his era fighting for the supremacy of the heavens in total war.

I have shared how this story came into being. Now it is important to realize that we are in the midst of a great spiritual war. You are invited to contact me at the following e-mail address: SixtusXystusVI@tutamail.com. May this primer on Revelation grant you the understanding which you seek.

Image of an angel similar to the one that
manifested itself after my prayer.

The Religious Retreat Chapel in Seoul, South Korea where Chaplain Clemens encountered an angel in 2006.

AUTHOR'S NOTE TO
THE THIRD EDITION

Dedicated to Douglas Carver, Executive
Director of Chaplains,
The North American Mission Board,
Southern Baptist Convention

"The fear of the Lord is the beginning of wisdom, and
the knowledge of the Holy One is understanding."
Proverbs 9:10 NAS

K NOWLEDGE IS FROM THE PAST; IT IS wisdom that grants us an understanding of the future. The first edition of "A Coming Of Truth" was released on 2 April 2008. During this time, I was an active-duty Army chaplain deployed with the 101st Airborne Division to the war in Afghanistan.

The book recounting my vision was received with controversy. Upon release it circled the globe within two months. It soon found me out on the rugged battlespace of Regional Command (RC) East.

This communication made me a target. Persecution would follow. The premise of my book has made for powerful enemies.

I was later to be eliminated from the Chaplain Corps. A suspicious secret "Controlled" promotion being made in my place by the Chief of Chaplains on the Fiscal Year 2011 Major promotion list. This is how the Army Chaplain Corps eats its own.

Twenty years after my vision, this renewed edition provides a glimpse into an upcoming spiritual struggle. This book will be received in different ways. Perhaps now it will be better accepted by a mass audience that senses something catastrophic is drawing near.

In the End Times, the Devil is planning an incursion upon the highest seat of Christendom. Lucifer's unholy mission is to mislead and destroy God's faithful. His agent of destruction is called the Antichrist. The Scriptures give us a vital but confusing clue to his identity.

This enemy is a powerful man whose name can be understood through numerology. We are told that his name equates to the number 666. Our reckoning will reveal the meaning of that title. In this Biblical summary you will learn of Satan's cunning plan for spiritual conquest.

My vision and its original interpretation still have value. The man I wrote about is now dead. Cardinal Vallejo's qualifications were unique. He was a dynamic figure unknown to me until I received my vision back in 2005.

The first book mentioning him commanded an online price of $3,500 during the conclave in which he was considered for Pope. All hell broke loose for me during this time. I would endure a period of longsuffering after the release of this material. In the end I would feel like Jonah after his mission to Ninevah.

This is a spiritual puzzle which has attracted the attention of many believers. The Antichrist spirit is far from dead. After many requests, it is time to reprint this book for the multitudes.

Watch & Pray,
Jeffrey Clemens

FOREWORD

"The testimony of the Lord is sure, making wise the simple."
Psalm 19:7 NAS

WE LIVE IN A FALLEN WORLD STRICKEN with religious discord and unending military conflict. The world yearns for a peacemaker. Someone who will transcend the differences of culture and faith. An individual who will serve as a reconciliatory force to unite all of humanity.

But where to find such a figure? This ecumenical mission can only be met by one office with a global reach. It is that of the mother church of Rome.

A future Bishop of Rome possessing incredible charisma is just the antidote for healing a world in turmoil. Someone who can unite the world's churches, and dialogue with those of the Jewish, and Muslim religions. In 2008 I released a book on such a figure which caused me considerable trouble in the Army Chaplain Corps.

The Revelation to John will serve as our guide. His account is a radical book that will test our limits of reason and faith. In his vision, John shares a very different world from which we live today. The living hell to come known as the New World Order is before us. By reading this primer on Revelation, you will be prepared for the greatest spiritual deception of all time.

The Bible cautions us that even God's elect will fall prey to Lucifer's debauchery. Our collective free will determines the future to come. This timeline is malleable. Do not yield to evil. Satan's deep and ancient plan for spiritual dominance is not to be underestimated.

The danger I warned about is still present. The figure I wrote about has passed into history. Consider this vision as a template. It will serve as a model for the grand deceiver yet to come whose final office contains the characters 666.

INTRODUCTION

"...for even Satan disguises himself as an angel of light,"
2 Corinthians 11:14 NAS

S ATAN IS BOLD, BUT HIGHLY PREDICTABLE. As a fallen angel he is prone to use light in his arsenal of deceit. It is a deadly snare for his spiritual traps, as "a liar and murder from the beginning." John 8:44 NAS.

I want to share with you a story from the late Warren Burke holder of Bedford, Virginia. In the 1950's he was the Sunday School Superintendent of New Prospect, my first church. He was long since retired and bent with age when we first met in 1991.

Pointing with his cane to the front door of the country church, he gave me a lesson in evil. In his quiet and folk-like manner, Warren mentioned that "Most people think of the devil as wearing a red suit, with horns, and having a pitchfork, and a tail. Nothing could be further from the truth. Satan would be the most handsome and worldly man you could ever meet, and you would want to be just like him!"

It has been thirty years since Warren shared these thoughts with me. His memory and words still remain vibrantly set in my mind. As a fledging mountain minister, he learned me up.

My task is to reveal the devil's business. Satan desires to be worshipped as God. The only place he can steal this devotion is from the churches of the world. There will be no pitchforks, or horns used in this spiritual attack, only the ruse of the shepherd.

You don't have to be a theologian to study this manuscript. The format is easy. I have recorded my vision for you and made it plain. Use it as you will and maintain your vigilance. Keeping alive the great expectancy of the Second Coming of Jesus Christ.

THE WAR FOR WORSHIP

"I will make myself like the Most High."
Isaiah 14:14 NAS

THESE ARE THE HAUGHTY WORDS THAT LED to the angelic revolt in heaven. They came from the corrupted heart of the fallen angel Lucifer. Desiring equality with God, the "light bearer" led a a failed rebellion for spiritual supremacy.

In defeat, Lucifer and one third of the angelic host would be eternally banished from heaven. Their wicked ways imprisoning them upon the lower realm of earth. Here they await their judgment until the end of the age.

This conflict is the first recorded act of warfare in history. Today this war for unseen worship continues in its full intensity. It remains the definitive battle between the forces of light and darkness.

The Scriptures reminds us that even in this lower state, Satan remains quite treacherous. The Biblical prophets have forewarned us of Lucifer's plans. We are to be on watch and pray.

Satan's spiritual mischief is to mislead the faithful with an imposter before the return of Christ. We know of this figure as the Antichrist. It is a term denoting one who either opposes or impersonates Christ. This false messiah is to be empowered directly from the lower realms of hell.

When it is allowed, Lucifer will install his mysterious Antichrist into a position of great authority. From this seat of power, the enemy will seek to deceive and destroy all of mankind. This man, whom our world will welcome as a savior will later prove himself to be our archenemy. His unholy mission is to deny Jesus and claim to be God. Ultimately, he will demand worship from the world under the penalty of death.

The prophecies of the Last Days are to prepare us for his rising. For the safekeeping of your soul, this evil must be revealed. God's living and amazing Word tells us how.

> "Here is wisdom. Let him who has understanding
> calculate the number of the beast, for the number is that
> of a man; and his number is six hundred and sixty-six."
> Revelation 13:18 NAS

Behind these three numbers lurks a master of intrigue, and mass destruction. The sex of which is that of a male. He will be disguised and fully backed by Satan. His unholy mission is to to wage a spiritual war for supremacy against the People of God.

The sequence of these three characters of sixes provides a positive match to the Antichrist. Each digit does in fact represent a physical name. However, it is not a regular birth name, or is it a name taken at this time. But rather a title pertaining to the future.

The number 666 is an ingenious cipher. For centuries, its encoded namesake has defied analysis. A vision I received in 2005 would reveal its incredible source.

It is a name composed of two ancient languages sequenced by Roman numerals. The languages of the past being used to warn us of a future threat. Once the Antichrist selects this title there can be no doubt about his motives or identity.

Take this personal testimony to heart in your preparation for the tribulation to come. It is my belief, and I am led to share it. To God be the glory.

MISSION

"And all who dwell upon the earth will worship him."
Revelation 13:8 NAS

IN HIS TIME, THE POWER OF THIS entity will be supreme. He will have dominion over the entire world. This is not a mere secular leader as some would surmise. Such a role demanding worship would come from the highest religious order.

Our spiritual mission is to reveal the 666 of Revelation. The following summary will give you the ability to recognize his plans for global rule. We are to be cautioned that Lucifer can conceal himself and recite Scripture for his own purpose. The same tactics will also be employed by his Antichrist.

This text is written as a simple warning. The information which it contains is necessary for its season of fulfillment. This is something that you and your loved ones must know.

May this account not be considered an attack against the Roman Catholic Church, or those who faithfully serve it. That is not my intention. My sole purpose is to bear the truth of the prophetic witness of Jesus Christ. This alone is my goal.

THE SIGN OF JONAH

"When God saw their deeds, that they turned
from their wicked way, then God relented
concerning the calamity which he had declared
He would bring them. And He did not do it."
Jonah 3:10 NAS

Does the Antichrist event have to happen? Is it even remotely possible to avoid the tribulation of these foretold days? The Old Testament story of Jonah continues to hold some powerful lessons for us.

In this brief book, the citizens of Nineveh were convinced by Jonah to forsake their sins. In so doing, God's wrath was extinguished. Their infamous city spared destruction. A sincere repentance would win them a reprieve from judgment.

When tested by His enemies, Jesus recounted the story of Jonah. In the Gospel of Matthew 12:38-41, Jonah's three days and three nights in the belly of a sea monster, reflected that of the entombed Jesus. The resurrection of Jesus three days later proving His identity as the Son of God.

With an insatiable curiosity we also yearn for a sign. The Antichrist prophecy will be to our spiritual detriment unless it is properly heeded. Like Jonah it requires a supernatural vision to perceive this danger, and a God granted wisdom to prepare for it.

No one else can spare you from this upcoming threat. Jesus is our only and everlasting hope to defeat the works of Satan. The blood of the Lamb of God will grant us certain victory. We either choose to obey Jesus Christ or suffer Satan's agent of destruction. This is our approaching struggle and a coming of truth. For the sake of eternity, we all must choose wisely.

THE GREATEST GENERATION

A time for war, and a time for peace."
Ecclesiastes 3:8 NAS

THE PREMISE OF THIS BOOK IS THAT of spiritual warfare. As a Soldier I was privileged in life to befriend actual heroes from our nation's wars. My most interesting friends were men and women who flew military aircraft in the Second World War.

Satan is called "the prince of the power of air" in Ephesians 2:2. The first part of my vision takes place in the heavenly realms with an air battle from World War II. To better understand this imagery I must share a fighter pilot story.

The message came back to me like an echo from my computer. "I'm still here thanks to your Boss, come and see me." The Holy Spirit led me to contact a brave man named Bill Overstreet of Roanoke, Virginia. I had read about him in Brigadier General Bud Anderson's book *To Fly And Fight*. Our first meeting was in cyberspace; later Bill and I became close personal friends.

At this time Bill was nearing the age of 80. During World War II he was a P-51 fighter pilot. Bill was an original "Yoxford Boys" pilot with the famed 357th Fighter Group based out of Leiston, England. His unit was remarkable. The 357th produced more ace pilots than any other fighter group in the 8th Air Force.

The man who opened his door to me was beyond modest. His first words to me were "All I want is for Eddie Simpson to be remembered." Captain Simpson was a close friend of his who died a heroic death on his last mission in August of 1944. I would honor Bill's request. In time I would further learn of Captain Overstreet's remarkable wartime service.

Born in 1921, Bill was a prime example of the courage and strength that was represented In Tom Brokaw's book "*The Greatest Generation*."This was a man who at age 23 downed a German Me-109 fighter aircraft through the Eiffel Tower before D-Day in 1944. In understanding the battles of Bill's generation, we can also defeat the evil spirits inhabiting the air.

Fighter pilot Bill Overstreet's incredible action at the Eiffel Tower was considered a spiritual sign of victory by the French Resistance during World War II.

MY VISION

"from visions of the night."
Job 4:13 NAS

This picture represents the P-51 Mustang aircraft
as seen in my vision from the 357th Fighter
Group. https://toflyandfight.com/heroes/

My first vision came late on the evening of 19 April 2005. On the television news, Cardinal Ratzinger had just announced himself as Pope Benedict XVI. I would be totally amazed by the impressions that came to me that evening as I prepared for sleep.

While staying as a guest at Bill Overstreet's home, I viewed a dozen P-51 Mustang fighters flying a combat mission. This projection was in color. It seemed like I was watching a silent movie from the past.

Nearing the enemy, the Mustang pilots maneuvered for battle. The flight leaders and their wingmen peeled off to attack. Their movements were quick and precise.

The American planes were painted in a Royal Air Force (RAF) green. A bold checkerboard pattern of yellow and red markings surrounding their cowlings. These aircraft had the markings of Bill's unit, the 357th Fighter Group. Their overall drab green paint scheme dating this action to the summer of 1944.

I then saw the Mustangs head-on from the perspective of the enemy. Closing within range, the Mustang pilots opened fire. Bursts of light were visible from their wings. The air was filled with lead. Their fifty caliber machine gun bullets reaching out to target.

There was no time to think, no glamour, just teamwork. Each man's fate depended completely on the other. They were of one mind engaged in battle. These pilots were flying and fighting in the realm of angels. This is what I saw.

The second vision immediately followed in black and white. It was not of the past, but of the future. There was a dominant figure of a man centered upon a stage in white. He was dressed as the pope, but without a cross. His identity was completely unknown to me.

At an intermediate distance behind him was a completed stone wall. Two bodies stood shoulder to shoulder against it. They both were dressed like the first figure, wearing miters. Their ashen gray faces frozen in the repose of death. Their features too distant to properly identify them.

I then took notice of this future pope. A man in his late seventies stood before me. A fierce countenance marked his face. His chin looked as if it were hewn from stone. There was no warmth to him. His eyes were intently evil and monster-like.

I was viewing a hologram. A wicked statue that could talk. It was a dreadful figure to look upon. It literally sickened me to observe it. The image before me was that of a beast from Revelation. It was absolutely dreadful.

Within seconds, the vision ended. Never in my life had I witnessed something so horrible! Those eyes were bent on manipulation. Their purpose was to survey and destroy; his being craving for worship. I memorized his facial features in this scant time.

That night I was granted a vision of the Antichrist spirit in his full terror. I saw a future pope who was literally a monster. It was revoting. Regardless of the controversy, it is time once more to release this book and expose the Devil's false messiah.

INTERPRETATION

"For nothing is hidden, except to be revealed; nor has anything been secret, but that it should come to light.
Mark 4:22 NAS

IN THE FIRST PART OF MY VISION, I witnessed the violence of aerial warfare. A dogfight is an intense conflict of man and machine. The enemy must be watched carefully. All movements are to be predicted and countered in a duel to the death.

From my many conversations with Bill Overstreet, I finally realized the full significance of the Mustang. The P-51 was the fighter for victory. This weapon arrived at the decisive hour to shift the balance of power in World War II. The men who flew it, literally altered history.

In the same spirit, we are also called into action for control of the heavens. The demonic battle before us will be a vicious struggle, much like a dogfight. Once more the epicenter of action being that of Europe.

In the second projection I viewed pure incarnate evil. The figure before me was completely possessed by the demonic. This was no ordinary man, but the beast, the most deadly being ever to walk the face of the earth.

It was almost unbelievable. In the second projection, I saw the perfect deception. The Holy Spirit had chosen this time to expose the approaching Antichrist in the guise of a future pope.

I was initially surprised by the figure before me. Pope Benedict XVI would step aside and not die in office. Pope Francis has since passed. Now we have Pope Leo XIV.

The man that I saw was later considered for the position of pope. His name was, His Eminence, the Cardinal Carlos Amigo Vallejo of Spain. Fortunately, this did not happen. The first book blocked him from this role. Our next chapter speaks of his person.

SIXTUS XYSTUS VI THE 666

Sixtus Xystus	I	117-125
Sixtus Xystus	II	257-258
Sixtus Xystus	III	432-440
Sixtus Xystus	IV	1471-1484
Sixtus Xystus	V	1585-1590

THE CIPHER OF REVELATION 13:18 CAN NOW be understood in the following manner. The numbers 666 would represent the last pope to bear the name Sixtus. By the grace of God what I wrote about did not happen. However, this scenario remains an active one.

Cardinal Vallejo was a Franciscan. Throughout the entire history of the Roman Catholic Church there have only been five popes chosen from this order. The last pope being Sixtus Xystus V from 1585-1590.

Upon selection each pope names himself. Traditionally a title is taken from within their own religious order. Each succeeding pope then receives a number. It is placed at the end of their title to designate their new identity.

Sixtus is a Roman name. In the past, it meant a sixth child. Five former popes are also known by this name. We have yet to see a successor to the title of Sixtus since 1590. Truly, it is an ominous thought.

If he was selected, it would have been Vallejo's destiny to claim the title Sixtus Xystus VI. This title literally means 666. Sixtus is Latin for six, and Xystus is Greek for six. The Roman numeral VI also equals the number six.

The mysterious identity of John's anticipated Antichrist will be revealed once this title is selected. The enemy is bound to do so by God's living Word. This is the promised wisdom to be granted by breaking the Revelation code.

Sixtus VI will also be known as Xystus VI. Do not be misguided, When the Antichrist assumes his final office he will be known by these multiple titles.

Cardinal Vallejo was born on August 23, 1934. He was no stranger to power. His career within the mother church had been nothing less than brilliant.

On 15-16 January 2008 Cardinal Vallejo was featured as a keynote speaker for the first forum of the Alliance Of Civilizations (AOC). This gathering of over 500 world leaders in Madrid was to promote cross-cultural understanding, pluralism, and conflict resolution for the United Nations.

Cardinal Vallejo had earlier served as the Archbishop of Tanger, Morocco from 1972-1982. His 1,600 Catholics safely practiced their religion in an interfaith environment; surrounded by four million Muslims. This experience had granted Cardinal Vallejo a noteworthy sensitivity to the nuances of the Muslim culture.

Cardinal Vallejo was also a skilled diplomat who had served as a mediator between nations. He had been recognized on a worldwide level for his diplomatic prowess in conflict resolution. Vallejo's credentials are in fact impeccable. This international figure was preordained to lead.

No small subject fell outside Vallejo's interest. This Cardinal was a master of all forms of communication. He was a gifted orator and prolific author who penned the account *"Christians And Muslims."* A book very much speaking of our time.

Before joining the Order of Friars Minor (O.F.M.) he studied medicine. Later he would round out his studies with multiple Ph.Ds. One in psychology, and the other in philosophy.

Cardinal Vallejo of course did not become pope. However, his background is significant. The qualities that he possessed would make for a world leader of considerable ability and power. The title of a future Sixtus remaining open until its Biblical fulfillment.

**Cardinal Carlos Amigo Vallejo who
appeared in my vision (1934-2022)**

WARS AND RUMORS OF WARS

"And you will be hearing of wars and rumors of wars;
see that you are not frightened. For those things
must take place, but that is not yet the end."
Matthew 24:6 NAS

WE ARE NOT TO BE AFRAID OF actual wars and the hearsay of further conflict. It is time to share two other projections which came upon me in the Spring of 2007. Their impressions remain quite sharp regarding a future surprise attack against Iran.

The first spiritual communication was that of millions of voices risen in shock and unison. "My God! We don't need another war! We don't even want this one!"

I knew this was the American People's response to the announcement of yet another war they had been deceived into fighting. Just like the disastrous campaigns of Iraq and Afghanistan. Later I would dream of the strike,

From a vantage point high up in the heavens, I looked down upon Iran. It was a cloudless and moonless night. I could see Persia perfectly outlined by its surrounding neighbors.

Within moments I saw segments of white light moving upon the Persian Gulf. There were a multitude of them. I watched them penetrate on inland, to the North and central parts of the country. Next, I saw huge explosions blanketing Iran.

The country was hit in a shock and awe attack, much like Iraq in 2003. This premeditated attack was an all-out assault against Iran. The ruin was great. This is what I witnessed. Such an attack will lead to a vicious war in which the people will beg for peace.

Iran's Nighttime Glow from Space- Backiee

A NEW HOLY
ROMAN EMPIRE

"A time to tear apart."
Ecclesiastes 3:7 NAS

The European Union Flag – a banner of destruction

A NEW UNITED STAES OF EUROPE IS EMERGING before our very eyes. This will not be a Eurozone, like the troubled European Union. For in the future Europe will have a greater power and influence through the creation of a new world bank and digital currency.

In October of 2011 the Vatican's Justice and Peace Department released papers calling for worldwide financial reforms. It seeks "universal jurisdiction" through "supranational authority." The goal of which is world governance through taxation and a new currency unit.

We are approaching a new paradigm. America is the world's greatest debtor nation. The dollar as a currency is dying. Once dead, the United States will lose its sovereignty.

The old economic model will be completely finished. In this power vacuum, Europe will take charge. Sixtus will then have absolute control through an Artificial Intelligence (A.I.) based cashless financial system.

The symbol of the new Europe is a series of twelve gold stars. They are positioned in the shape of a crown, centered on a blue banner. This symbol represents a revived Holy Roman Empire. The only figure missing is that of Caesar.

History is important in understanding the Bible. We are literally revisiting the powers of ancient Rome in the present. God has warned us in His Holy Scriptures of this time and place.

This new Rome will be the kingdom of the Antichrist. We will witness the final papacy of Peter acting as the Roman. The false image of a man posing as Peter, fully corrupted by the decadence of Rome.

BY PEACE HE SHALL DESTROY

"And he will destroy many while they are at ease."
Daniel 8:25 NAS

THE TACTIC OF PEACE CAN ALSO BE utilized to cause further destruction. History is marked by numerous armistices which have led to future slaughters. Ultimately treaties of disarmament take away the ability of nations to resist and defend themselves.

Daniel's warning is to be kept alive with a special watchfulness. We are to be on guard for a false peacemaker. Someone who would grant us a misleading sense of security before he destroys us.

An ecumenical platform is ideal for a peacemaker. The chosen symbol of the future Sixtus will be that of a dove.

The 666 will later decimate his opposition through the peace process. The masses once asleep will not perceive their danger until it is too late. After their ability to resist is dismantled; many will perish without a fight.

Vatican Dove Peace Stamp

FALSE SIGNS AND WONDERS

"And the whole earth was amazed
and followed after the beast."
Revelation 13:3 NAS

THE MINISTRY OF SIXTUS WILL MIMIC THAT of Jesus Christ. Superior in the powers of mind and speech, Sixtus will seduce the world. In time false signs and wonders will accompany his person. He will even taste death and then seem to rise from the dead.

Revelation 13:3 describes his fatal head wound being healed. I can picture Sixtus on life support after being shot in the head by an assassin's bullet. The fallen pope having no brain activity until evil incarnates into his near-death form.

Satan will take this opportunity to raise his counterfeit Christ from the appearance of death. This pseudo-resurrection of Sixtus by the powers of darkness, stunning the world. This being the Devil's attempt to imitate the raising of Jesus from the dead.

Fully possessed by Satan, Sixtus now assumes the identity of the Antichrist. Sixtus Xystus VI the 666 is then unleashed for his mission of terrible destruction. A great authority being granted to the 666 for a period of forty-two months (Revelation 13:5).

THE TEMPLE

"There is but one God, and one God only. Let
us build one tabernacle to serve Him."
Pope Sixtus Xystus VI

JERUSALEM IS TO BE HIS PRIZE. To consolidate his power, Sixtus will move the mother church to its point of origin in the Holy City. Delicate negotiations will then be won through his person. He will secure the necessary cooperations to rebuild the third Jewish temple on its original site.

The temple will be completed within the span of a year on Mount Moriah. The construction materials have long since been prefabricated, strategically placed for rapid assembly. Its highly skilled masons awaiting their summons to build. The priestcraft already identified and pretrained for their sacrificial duties. Their instruments and implements of worship also having been created awaiting their sacred usage.

Once more, the temple will be utilized for worship. The Jewish priests will make their regular sacrifices as recorded in Biblical times. However, their joy will be short-lived.

At the moment of his choosing, Sixtus will abolish their rituals. He will then take "his seat in the temple of God, displaying himself as being God." Thus, fulfilling Paul's words from 2 Thessalonians 2:3-4.

The shock will be immense as the Christians, Jews, and Muslims recognize their fatal error. The temple reconstruction will be for the benefit of Satan. After having seized this prime objective, Sixtus will then brutally rout his religious opposition.

The temple will then be desecrated. Swine will be slaughtered and burned upon the holy altar. With great arrogance, the 666 will proclaim himself the Most High, demanding allegiance and worship under the penalty of death.

Third Jewish Temple image by John Reve 2010

POSITIVE ID MICROCHIPS

"...and he provides that no one should be able to buy
or to sell, except the one who has the mark, either the
name of the beast, or the number of his name."
Revelation 13:17 NAS

To further his dominance, Sixtus will alter the medium of exchange in the global economy. Fiat currency will be made obsolete. To buy, sell, or trade, everyone will be forced to receive a "mark" (Revelation 13:16-17).

This mark will be placed in either the right hand or triceps. A secondary site will also be the forehead. For those physically unable to tolerate this procedure, the mark can either be placed in a necklace or worn as a bracelet.

At first its use will be voluntary, then mandated. All sincere Christians should not receive the microchip. This form of allegiance can only lead to our spiritual suicide,

The mark of the beast will provide for worldwide tracking, and the elimination of all personal liberty. The technology is available today in a device deceptively called Positive ID. It is a sub-dermal implant commonly used for animal identification.

The Positive ID microchip is about the size of a grain of rice. It is placed in the human body by a syringe. It is essentially a radio transmitter that can be tied into technology. In time it will be used for all financial transactions and make for our digital enslavement.

The rich and the poor who accept this mark will surrender their free will to the demonic. The final fate of those chipped is eternal damnation. To voluntarily be microchipped makes you an enemy of God; the cost of which is your very soul.

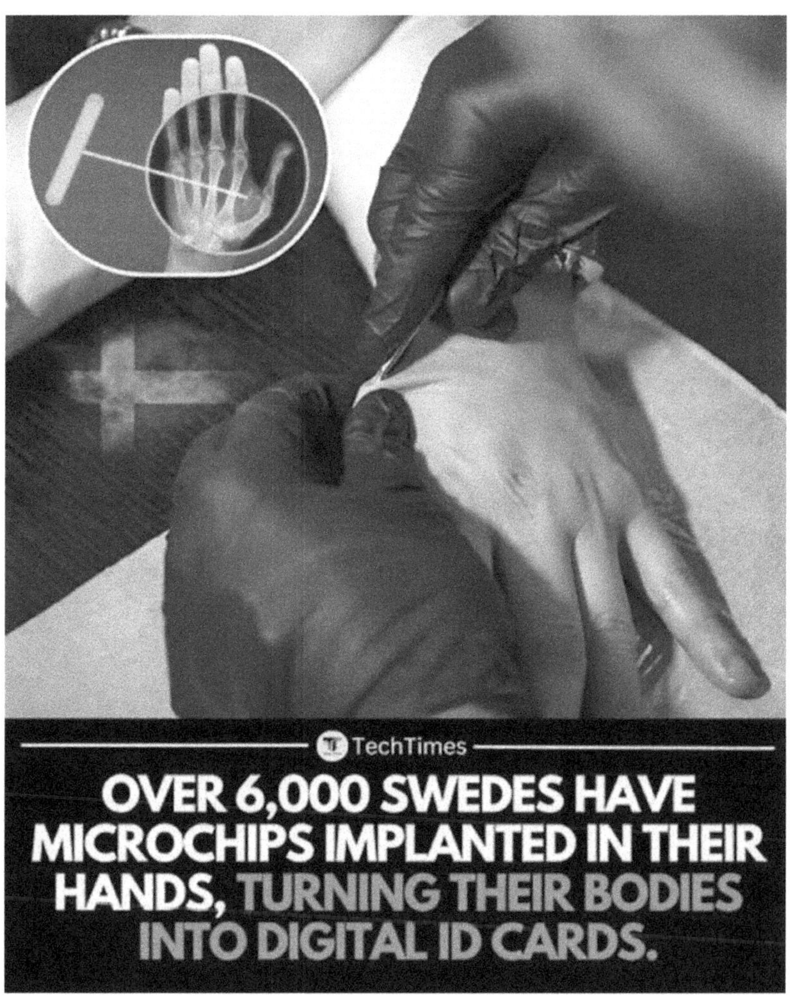

Microchipping for identification, banking, and key access.

TRIBULATION, RAPTURE, & THE SECOND COMING OF JESUS CHRIST

"...for then there will be great tribulation,
such as has not occurred since the beginning
of the world until now, nor ever shall."
Matthew 24:21 NAS

W ITH THE POSITIVE ID AND AN A. I. digital economic system in place, our spiritual freedoms will be eliminated. This is Satan's master plan. Those challenging the authority of the 666 will face intense persecution and death. There will be no sanctuary or quarter for his enemies in this world.

It will be a time of incredible hardship. As people's hearts become extinguished and grow cold, we are warned by Jesus in the following words:

> "Then they will deliver you up to tribulation, and kill you, and you will be hated by all nations on account of my name. And at that time many will fall away and will betray one another and hate one another. And many false prophets will arise, and mislead many. And because lawlessness is increased, most people's love will grow cold. But the one who endures to the end, it is he who shall be saved. And this gospel of the kingdom shall be preached in the whole world for a witness to all the nations, and then the end shall come," Matthew 24:9-14 NAS

This is a critical message for all believers. It is not a false feel-good prosperity gospel. Christ's warning of such suffering and death is indeed grim. Unfortunately, from the pulpits of today this message is something you rarely hear of.

Many Christians are under the false impression that they will be "raptured" away from this hostile spiritual environment. That in the future they will be magically lifted up from the physical to a spiritual form. The Church it seems is promised a free ride to heaven before the tribulation period even begins.

It certainly sounds simple. There is no preparation to avoid this crisis and the rewards are surreal. But this runs counter to what Jesus has shared with us. So, what is the truth of the matter?

The facts will surprise you. The rapture was not a belief in American Christianity until the early 1860's. This belief originated from a man of Anglo-Irish descent named John Nelson Darby.

Darby made five missionary journeys to America between 1862 and 1877. His self-invented teachings of a pre-tribulation rapture became quickly absorbed into American religious thought. Interestingly enough, his theology then found its way into the Scofield Reference Bible. The pre-tribulation rapture has since become ingrained into mainstream Christianity despite its faulty reasoning.

Today this false belief continues to bring tremendous confusion to the modern church. People have heard this story over their entire lives. They sincerely believe that they will not have to suffer the Devil's tribulation.

According to our passage in Matthew those who profess Christ are to remain as His witnesses during this hellish trial. The angels will not gather the faithful until after the tribulation. Finally, a series of celestial signs will announce the Second Coming of Jesus Christ in Matthew 24:29-31. This harvesting of souls being what most people know by the non-biblical term "rapture."

The moment of Christ's return is the most closely guarded secret of God's universe. Once released by God, Jesus and His Army from heaven are to engage the enemy, The scheme for spiritual conquest by the Antichrist is then completely doomed. The beast will then be seized and thrown into a "lake of fire" Revelation 19:20.

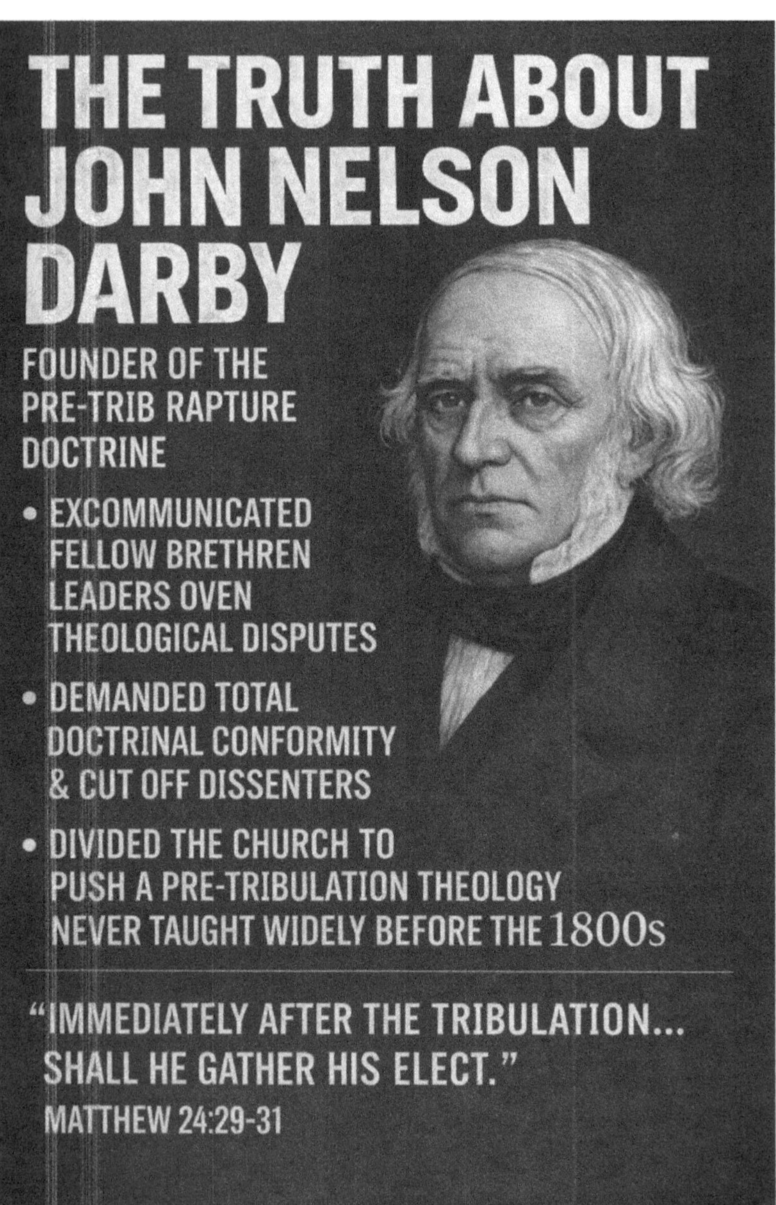
THE TRUTH ABOUT JOHN NELSON DARBY
FOUNDER OF THE PRE-TRIB RAPTURE DOCTRINE
• EXCOMMUNICATED FELLOW BRETHREN LEADERS OVEN THEOLOGICAL DISPUTES
• DEMANDED TOTAL DOCTRINAL CONFORMITY & CUT OFF DISSENTERS
• DIVIDED THE CHURCH TO PUSH A PRE-TRIBULATION THEOLOGY NEVER TAUGHT WIDELY BEFORE THE 1800s
"IMMEDIATELY AFTER THE TRIBULATION... SHALL HE GATHER HIS ELECT."
MATTHEW 24:29-31

55

**Image from Revelation Revolution of Jesus
returning in the clouds with His angelic army.**

JESUS IS OUR COMING OF TRUTH

"...abide in Him, so that when He appears, we
may have confidence and not shrink away
from Him in shame at His coming."
1 John 2:28 NAS

U NLESS MANKIND REPENTS OF ITS SINS, WE will suffer Satan's
son of destruction. This is a personal decision which we
all must make. Remember Jonah's mission to Nineveh? The
future that we invite also hinges upon the same choice.

There is only one true hope, and His name is Jesus. No
mere man can claim His title or successfully impersonate His
greatness. He alone is our Savior and King.

Revelation 19:10 tells us that "the testimony of Jesus is
the spirit of prophecy." It is in this spirit that I submit my

recollections to you. The vision I received is of a future leader of Rome named Sixtus Xystus VI the 666.

No one would ever expect Satan's spiritual attack to take place at the highest office of the Vatican. This is what the Revelation to John is communicating to us. To be forewarned is to be forearmed.

May this brief account give you the needed awareness to prepare for this time of great testing. To be complacent is to invite personal and spiritual tragedy. Trust only in Jesus to defeat the works of the enemy through His victory over sin and death. You are sealed in His blood for eternity.

The triumph of the human spirit is represented
by the courage of Captain Edward K Simpson,
363rd FS, Killed In Action 14 Aug 1944.
https://www.roaonoke8thairforce.
com/capt-edward-k-simpson

Home of record: East Orange, New Jersey

Eddie was such a likable easy-going person. He was a superb
pilot and a team member. Very dependable, always right there
where you wanted him all the time. He was officially credited
with 4 1/4 aerial kills. We were close friends.

While I was in the US for R & R during the summer of 1944,
Capt. Simpson was involved in a midair collision with squadron
mate Lt. Don Ferron, west of Sens, France. Lt. Ferron didn't make
it. Simpson survived the midair but was later killed by Germans
while attempting to escape with the French underground.
Brigadier General C.E. "Bud" Anderson, U.S.A.F. (1922-2024)

www.ingramcontent.com/pod-product-compliance
Lightning Source LLC
Chambersburg PA
CBHW050016040726

47599CB00014B/1407